Social Skills Activities for Today's Kids

AGES
10–11

Name:

Note to Parents

The activities in this book are designed to help your child think about social skills and how they can be used in everyday life at school, at a restaurant, or online, for example. Learning social skills will be an important part of your child having friendships and other meaningful relationships, as well as positive interactions with his or her peers and safe and responsible experiences online.

Provide support as your child does the activities. Discuss your child's feelings and thoughts and answer any questions your child has. Learning social skills can be challenging, so being patient and providing support as your child learns how to apply what he or she has learned to relationships and social situations is an important part of your child's experience.

Editorial Development: Monika Davies
Leslie Barnard Booth
Teera Robinson
Lisa Vitarisi Mathews
Copy Editing: Kathleen Jorgensen
Art Direction: Yuki Meyer
Cover Illustration: Dana Regan
Illustration: Bryan Langdo
Design/Production: Jessica Onken

EMC 3120

Evan-Moor Corporation
phone 1-800-777-4362, fax 1-800-777-4332.

10 Harris Court, Suite C-3, Monterey, CA 93940-5773. Printed in China.

CPSIA: Asia Pacific Offset Ltd, Kowloon, Hong Kong, China [10/2024]

002

CONTENTS

Making Friends

Contents continue on the next page.

Being at School

Contents continue on the next page.

Going Places

Out and About 72

At a Restaurant 87

At the Store 93

Contents continue on the next page.

Being Online

Making Friends

Making friends can be fun. There are things to think about when you are making new friends. There are things to think about when you have friends.

- ☆ You can think about how to introduce yourself.
- ☆ You can think about what to say to friends.
- ☆ You can think about how friends treat each other.
- ☆ You can think about having friends over to your home and going to your friends' homes.

It's not always easy to know what to say to make new friends or what to say to your friends. It's not always easy to know what to do with your friends. Thinking about these things can help you figure out what you are comfortable saying and doing in a friendship.

Page 8

Page 19

Page 30

Introducing Yourself

When you meet new people, you can introduce yourself. You might share your name with them or ask them a short question about themselves.

What steps do you like to take when you meet someone new? Look at the "stepping stones" on the left. Then choose which steps you would take and write one step on each stone on the right.

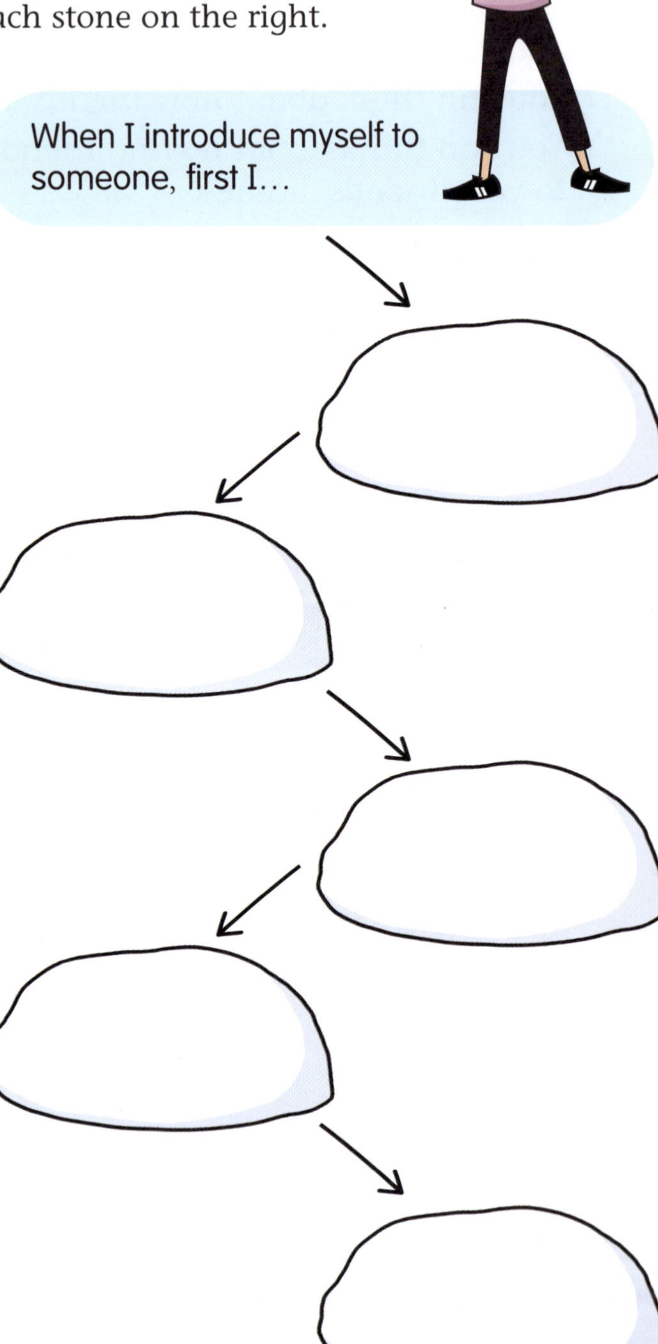

Asking People Questions

When you meet someone new, it can be helpful to ask him or her questions. Sometimes short or simple questions can help you get to know someone a little better.

You might ask different questions in different settings. Look at the pictures below. If you met new people in this setting, what question could you ask them?

You meet new people on the playground. What question could you ask them?

____

____

____

You meet new people at an art club. What question could you ask them?

____

____

____

You meet new people at summer camp. What question could you ask them?

____

____

____

Deeper Questions Activity

When you become friends with someone, it can be hard to always know what to talk about. Sometimes it's hard to think of topics that are interesting for everyone. One thing you can do is ask some deeper questions. When you ask people deep questions about themselves, you can learn a lot about them.

Use these conversation cards to learn more about a friend.

What You Need

- page 11
- pen or pencil
- scissors
- a friend

What You Do

1. Read the conversation cards on page 11. Which of these questions would you like to ask your friends? Draw a small star on all the cards with questions that you would ask.
2. On the blank cards, write your own deep questions to ask friends.
3. Cut out the cards you drew a star on and the ones with the questions you wrote.
4. Bring the conversation cards with you when you are going to be with a friend. Take turns choosing cards and asking each other questions. You can save the cards and use them with other friends.

What is your favorite meal to eat? Why is it your favorite?

If you could meet anyone in the world, whom would you meet? Why?

What is your favorite memory with your family?

What do you like best about yourself? What do you like least about yourself?

What are three things you are grateful for in your life?

If you could plan the perfect day, what would you be doing?

What do you think are the most important things about a friend?

What is the kindest thing someone has ever done for you?

What are two things you are afraid of?

Talk with Your Family

Respecting Rules at Your Friend's House

Sometimes you might want to go to a new friend's house. Many times, families have house rules. It is important to treat your friends with respect by respecting rules at their houses.

Talk with your parent. Brainstorm and write ways that you can respect the rules at your friends' houses.

How can I respect the rules at my friend's house?

When I arrive at someone's house, I will...

When I eat with others, I will...

If I feel confused about a rule, I will...

Some other ways I can show respect are...

Ways to Join In

When you meet new people, you might want to join them or get to know them. There are things you can say to people you don't know well so that you can make new friends and get to know them better.

Read the situations below and the things you could say.
Then write a √ by the things you would say if you were in that situation.

#1: Ask if you can join in.
You see a kid kicking a ball around the field. You like to play soccer, too. You can walk up to the kid playing and ask if you can play, too.

Things you could say:

1. Hey, I'm ______! Can I kick the ball around with you?
2. Hi there. Can I play, too?

#2: Talk about what you have in common.
You see a boy painting in the art room. He is painting a watercolor picture of hummingbirds. You also love to paint with watercolors. You can walk up to him and talk about what you have in common.

Things you could say:

1. I also love painting with watercolors. Can I paint with you?
2. I like the colors you are using. I have the same paint set as you!

#3: Say something nice.
While you are at a museum, you see a boy who is in your learning group at school. He is wearing bright yellow shoes. You think the shoes look cool, and you want to say something nice to let him know.

Things you could say:

1. Wow, your shoes are cool! Where did you get them?
2. Your shoes look awesome. I've never seen that shade of yellow before.

#4: Ask questions to start a conversation.
You see a new girl at your martial arts class. She looks like she might be new to town. You can walk up to her and ask questions to start a conversation.

Things you could say:

1. Hi there! Have you done this before, or this is your first time?
2. Hey, I'm ____. What's your favorite martial arts move?

#5: Tell how you are feeling.
You see a kid sitting alone at the fire at your camp. You do not know anyone else at the camp. You can walk up to the kid and share how you are feeling. He or she might feel the same way.

Things you could say:

1. I don't know anyone here. Can I sit with you?
2. This is my first time at camp, and I'm feeling a bit nervous. Is it okay if I sit here?

Friendship Practice

Making New Friends

You might feel nervous or awkward inviting someone to play, sit, or talk with you. It can help to think about what you would do and say ahead of time.

Read about each situation. Then answer the question.

You go to a pottery class to learn how to make a mug. It's your first time making pottery. You see a girl who looks friendly. She has a colorful backpack. She's alone, and so are you. Maybe you and she can be friends. What could you do next?

____

____

____

____

You go to a day camp during spring break. It is an improv workshop, and you are practicing how to tell a story to someone else. You see a boy who looks friendly. He is wearing a T-shirt with your favorite band's name on it. You would like to work on a story together and make a new friend. What could you do next?

ROCK IT UP!

____

____

____

____

You are starting a new diving class. You see a kid your age diving off the high board! You would like to talk to the kid after class and make a new friend. What could you do next?

____

____

____

____

You are at the park.You see a few kids who are having fun playing tag. You would like to play with them and make some new friends. What could you do next?

____

____

____

____

Talking with Parents

When you hang out with new friends, you might also meet their parents. What can you talk about with someone else's parent?

Look at the topics below. Circle the topics that you might choose to talk about with your friend's parent. Write an idea of your own.

I could talk about an activity I do with my friend, like baseball or dance class.

I could talk about what I'm learning in school or a homework assignment I'm working on with my friend.

I could talk about the weather, such as the huge snowfall we had last week.

I could ask him or her if there are any rules I should know about at their house.

____

____

____

What Do You Want in a Friend?

What is a friend? Think about what a friend does and says. Think about what you like about having friends.

Circle the hands that tell what you want a friend to do. Cross out the hands that tell what you don't want a friend to do. Then write in the blank hand to tell one more thing that makes a good friend.

I want a friend to . . .

- encourage me
- give me gifts
- tease me
- ask to copy my homework
- be honest with me
- make fun of my other friends
- listen when I'm sad
- have fun ideas
- help me when I have a problem
- like doing dangerous things
- make me laugh
- never say no to me

I Can Be a Friend

You can be a friend. You can help your friends by being kind to them, listening to them, and helping them in many ways.

Draw yourself below. Then look at page 21. Choose the words and pictures that show what kind of friend you want to be. Cut them out and glue them around the picture of you. You can also add your own words and pictures if you want to.

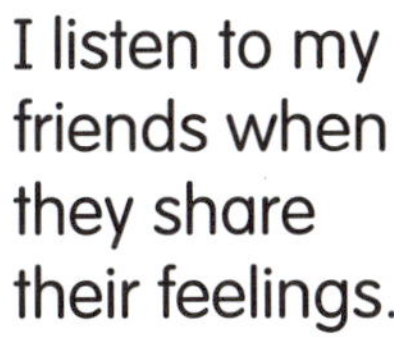

I listen to my friends when they share their feelings.

I encourage my friends when they are working really hard at something.

If my friends lose something, I try to help them find it.

I help my friends get up when they fall.

If someone is saying something hurtful about my friends, I tell the person to stop.

I notice when my friends are sad, and I try to help.

I carry things for my friends when their arms are full.

I ask my friends how they are feeling.

I have fun with my friends!

When I disagree with my friends, I try to talk with them calmly.

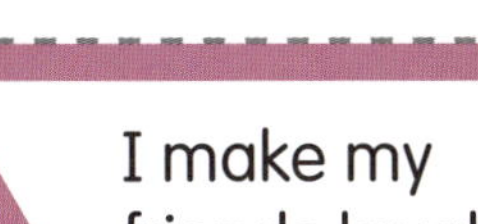

I make my friends laugh!

I tell my friends, "Good job!"

I greet my friends with a smile.

I cheer up my friends when they're sad.

Talk with Your Family

How Do I Keep My Friends?

Having friends is fun. It can also be difficult sometimes. People have to make choices every day, and sometimes these choices can affect their friends. Sometimes it helps to think about how you might handle certain situations. It could help to talk to your family about different situations, too.

Read the questions below with your parents. Talk about the answers.

What might make someone not want to be friends anymore?

What is okay and not okay for me to do to keep a friend?

- Is it okay to lie to impress my friends?
- Is it okay to give away my belongings as gifts?
- Should I do things that could get me in trouble or be embarrassing to make my friends laugh?

What if a friend makes me feel bad about myself sometimes?

Glitter Globe Gift

Sometimes friends make gifts for each other.
Make a glitter globe to give to one of your friends.

What You Need

- jar with a lid that can close tightly
- glitter
- water
- figurines or decorations that are waterproof (not metal) and can fit in the jar
- superglue or rubber cement
- materials to decorate the jar (optional)

What You Do

1. Use the glue to stick the figurines and decorations inside the bottom of the jar.
2. Let the glue dry.
3. Add glitter to the jar.
4. Fill the jar completely with water.
5. Carefully close the lid of the jar as tightly as you can.
6. If you want, decorate the jar.
7. Shake the jar to see the glitter float.
8. Give the glitter globe to one of your friends!

Empathy

When you have empathy, it means that you try to understand what other people might be feeling. Friends try to have empathy for each other.

Read the stories. Can you imagine how each person might be feeling? Draw faces to show what you think the person is feeling. Then write the name of the feeling or feelings.

Augustaf worked on his presentation on dolphins for two weeks. He took lots of notes. Finally, the day arrived for him to present to the class. He went to the front of the class. That's when he realized he'd forgotten his notes at home.

Augustaf

How is Augustaf feeling?

____

____

The teacher told the class to get into groups of 4 or 5. Everyone found a group except for Destiny. She asked to join a few groups, but they all said, "We're full."

Destiny

How is Destiny feeling?

____

____

Diego was enjoying his food in the school cafeteria. Then the kid next to him said, "Dude, your lunch stinks."

Diego

How is Diego feeling?

____

____

Hurt Feelings

Sometimes friends disagree or hurt each other's feelings. If you hurt a friend's feelings, you can work to make things better by saying you're sorry and doing things differently next time.

Look at the visual story.
Malcom is wearing a yellow shirt, and Emiliano is wearing a red shirt.

How do you think Emiliano is feeling? Circle one or more answers.

lonely angry embarrassed sad

in pain misunderstood left out

Draw what you think Malcom and Emiliano should do and say next.

Ups and Downs

Friends are kind and helpful to each other. But sometimes friendships have ups and downs. Friends sometimes hurt each other's feelings. Friends can talk about their problems with each other and try to work them out.

Read each situation below. Then color **yes** or **no** to answer the question.

Blanca left her water bottle at home. June tells her the office has extra water bottles if she needs one and offers to walk to the office with her.

Is June being a helpful friend?

yes ○ **no** ○

Antonio, Chris, and Dwayne share a table in their class. Chris reaches across the table and takes Dwayne's pencil. Dwayne asks for it back, but Chris ignores him. Then Antonio tells Chris to give it back. Chris doesn't respond.

Should Dwayne ask Chris why he is acting mean?

yes ○ **no** ○

Priscilla, Gabriana, and Azul are friends. At lunch they all sit together. Priscilla and Gabriana talk about the sleepover they are having on Friday. Azul is not invited. Azul sits quietly while they talk. She feels left out.

Should Azul let her friends know that they are hurting her feelings?

yes ○ **no** ○

Mikey was showing his friend Ian his watch when it fell and cracked. "You broke it!" Mikey yelled at Ian.

"Hey, Mikey, I know you're upset about the watch, but I didn't make it fall. We can get it fixed after school. Do you want me to see if my dad can take us?" asked Ian.

"Sorry. I know you didn't break it. Yeah, that would be great," said Mikey.

Was this a good way to talk it out?

yes ○ **no** ○

Friends Help

Friends help each other in different ways. Sometimes they help by listening, offering ideas, or saying something kind.

Read the situations. Draw a line matching each situation to the response a friend might give.

Oh, no! I spilled milk all over myself.

No worries. You can borrow mine.

Ugh. I just don't know what topic to do for my project.

I'm sorry that happened! I'll run and get some napkins!

Uh oh. I forgot my eraser at home.

What about dinosaurs? You love dinosaurs!

Read about the situation. Then write your own response from a friend.

This math question is so confusing.

Friend Poem

An acrostic poem has a word written from top to bottom. Each letter in the word starts a line of the poem. Each line of the poem describes this word. Here is an example:

Clever and soft
Always curling up on my lap
Tail twisting as she purrs

Think about what makes a good friend.
Write a poem that tells what the word **friend** means to you.

F ____________________

R ____________________

I ____________________

E ____________________

N ____________________

D ____________________

Things to Do with a Friend

When a friend comes over to your home, you might not know what to do at first. That's okay. You can think of things to do with a friend.

Brainstorm! Draw some games or activities you play at home. Include toys or other items you like to play with.

Now write a list of things you like to do at home. Look at your list. Circle which of these things might be fun to do with a friend.

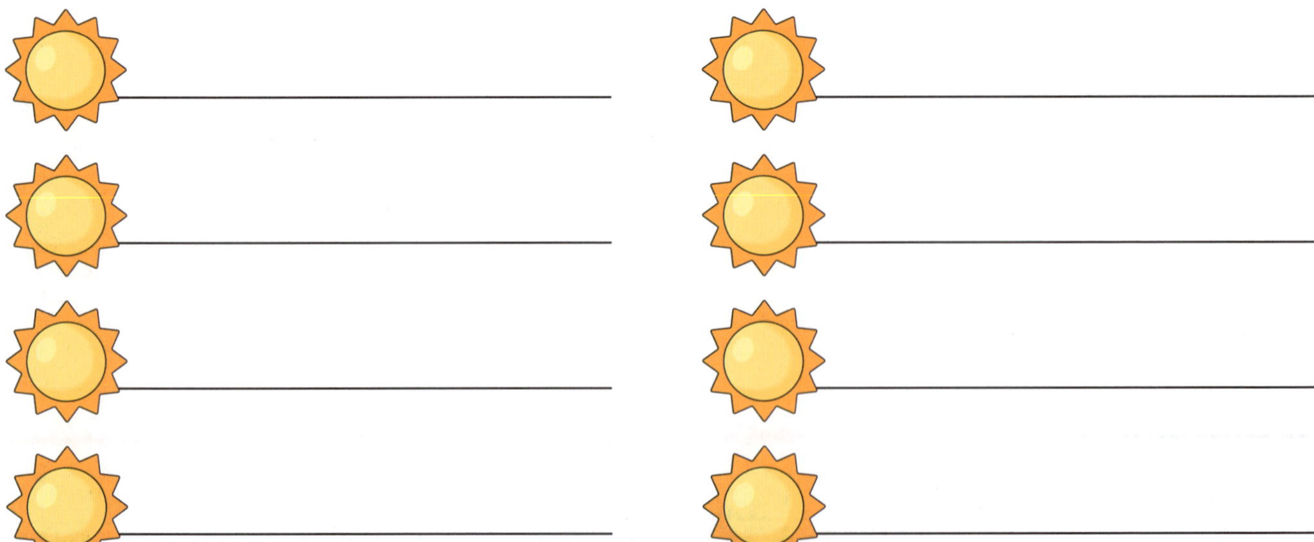

Explaining the Rules

Your friends might have rules at their houses. You might have different rules at your home. You can explain the rules of your house to your friends.

Read the House Rule.

House Rule

We ask permission before we use the computer.

Imagine that this is a rule at your home. You are having a new friend over to play. Your friend doesn't know the rules and starts to play games on your family computer. Think about what you would do. Then read the responses below. Circle the ones you think are best. Write an **X** to cross out responses you wouldn't use. Then make up your own response and write it in the blank speech bubble.

Setting Boundaries

Sometimes you might feel like telling your friends "no" or that you don't feel comfortable with something. That is okay. It is called setting boundaries. A boundary is like a line you draw to show what you are okay with and what you are not okay with. Everyone has boundaries. It's not always easy to say what your boundaries are, but it can help you be happier around your friends.

Read the story. Then do the activity.

Liz had her friend Cecilia at her house. They were listening to music in Liz's room. Cecilia started going through clothes in Liz's closet. "I like this," said Cecilia. "Oh, I do NOT like this! This is nice, and that is nice. Ah, this top is cute. I'm gonna take this top home and borrow it, okay?"

Liz did not like how Cecilia was going through all her clothes and saying what she thought. It hurt Liz's feelings when Cecilia said she didn't like something of hers. And Liz really didn't like that Cecilia said she'd borrow something without asking.

Which of these statements could Liz use to say that she has boundaries? Write a √ inside each speech bubble that would work.

I didn't actually ask you to go through my closet and tell me what you think about my clothes. Can we do something else?

I'd rather you ask if you can borrow something instead of just taking it.

I guess that's okay.

I'm glad you think I have some cute clothes.

Write one more thing Liz could say:

Read the story. Then do the activity.

Braden and Glenn were playing video games and snacking on popcorn. They had been playing for a while, and Glenn was thinking about going back to his own house soon. His older sister was coming home from college to hang out with the family for the weekend, and he was excited to see her.

"Hey, after this do you want to ride bikes?" asked Braden.

"Hmm, maybe, for a bit," said Glenn. "I also want to…"

"You should call your mom and ask if you can eat here tonight," Braden interrupted. "Or better yet, ask if you can spend the night!"

"Well, my sister's actually visiting this weekend," said Glenn.

"Oh, come on! My mom's making spaghetti. It's the best. And she makes French toast every Saturday morning, too!"

"It's just that…" started Glenn. But Braden interrupted him again!

"Well, I guess if you have to go home, you should. But then you HAVE TO come over tomorrow and Sunday. I still want to show you my dad's new camping gear, and there's a lot more stuff we didn't get to do."

Which of these statements could Glenn use to say that he has boundaries? Write a √ inside each speech bubble that would work.

Fine, I'll call my mom and ask her.

I like hanging out with you, but I already made plans for this weekend.

You're not listening to me. I am trying to tell you that my sister is visiting, so I have to go home tonight.

Write one more thing Glenn could say:

I'm sorry, I can't hang out this weekend. How about next weekend?

Friend Silhouette

When you have a friend over, you can make an art project about him or her. This project will show how unique your friend is and what you like about him or her.

What You Need

- pages 35–37
- pencil
- large posterboard
- scissors
- tape
- flashlight and someone to hold it
- wall you can tape posterboard onto
- a friend
- materials you can use to decorate, such as pictures you can cut out, cotton balls, markers, paint, pom-poms, beads, toothpicks, dried flowers, fabric, foil, glue, etc.

What You Do

1. Tape the posterboard to the wall so the top part is higher than your friend's height. Then ask your friend to stand in front of the posterboard, a few feet away from the wall. Your friend must stand sideways, or parallel to the wall and paper.
2. Ask someone to stand farther away from the wall and to shine the flashlight at your friend, but not in your friend's eyes. The goal is to use the light to create your friend's shadow on the posterboard so you can trace your friend's shadow.
3. Trace your friend's profile shadow.

What You Do, *continued*

4. Cut out the shadow you traced. After you cut it out, ask your friend to answer the questions on page 36.
5. Use your friend's answers from page 36 to decorate the cut-out silhouette. Use your friend's favorite colors. Cut and paste pictures that show things your friend likes. You may choose to use the pictures on page 37.
6. Show your friend's name or nickname somewhere on the silhouette. You can write the name, paint it, or cut and paste letters to make it.
7. Give the Friend Silhouette you made to your friend as a gift!
8. If you want, ask your friend to create a Friend Silhouette for you, too! Write your answers to the questions on page 36 on a separate sheet of paper.

Friend Silhouette Questions

Answer the questions.

What are your 3 favorite colors? Write the colors or show them inside the crayons.

What animal are you most like, and why? Or what animal do you like most and why?

What are your 3 favorite foods?

What is one of the most important things you want people to know about you?

Being at School

There are many things to think about when you are at school.

- ☆ You think about the things you need to do at school.
- ☆ You think about what to say to the kids and adults at school.
- ☆ You think about whom you want to play with and eat with at school.
- ☆ You think about the rules at school.

Sometimes it's hard to know exactly what to say and do in some situations at school. It might help to think about your feelings about the rules, people, and things that happen at school.

Page 40

Page 50

Page 65

Respecting Others

A lot of things happen during the school day. There are things you have to do and keep in mind. There are a lot of people and a lot of different personalities at school. As you go through your day, give yourself one simple rule to remember above all others: respect other people. Doing that will help you handle even difficult situations.

The social situations below happen every day at school. How do you respect others in each situation? Write and draw to show what you can do.

standing in line

saying something in a class discussion

walking in a crowded school hallway

working in a group of your classmates

Remove this chart and post it where you can see it.

These Healthy Habits
Show Your Classmates You Care

Use your arm or shoulder to cover your mouth when you cough or sneeze.

Wash your hands with soap and water.

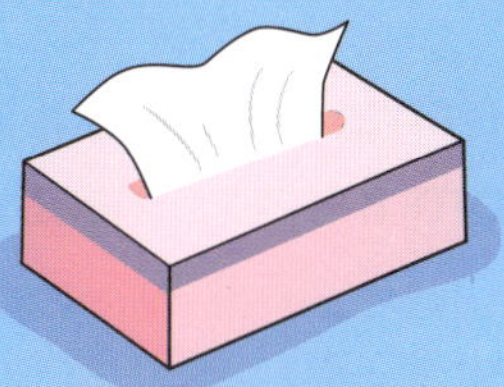

Use a tissue instead of your sleeve or hands.

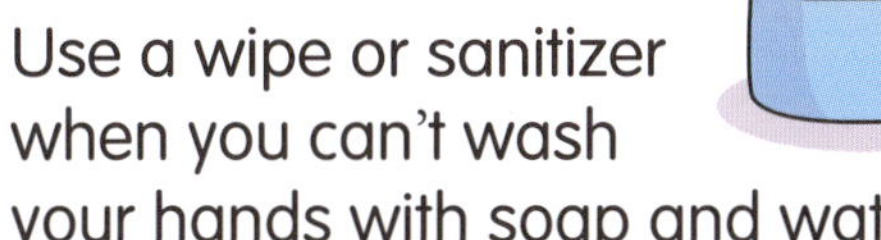

Use a wipe or sanitizer when you can't wash your hands with soap and water.

Stay home when you feel sick.

Do not put your mouth directly onto the water fountain spout.

Do not touch other kids' snacks or food.

Keep your distance from other people if they are coughing or sneezing.

Remove this chart and post it where you can see it.

Being a Respectful Classmate and Friend

Be yourself. Be honest about what you like and dislike.

Respect other people's personal space. Not everyone likes to be close to others.

Follow the examples of people you look up to who are responsible and kind.

Follow classroom rules.

Respect other people's belongings.

Listen when other people are speaking.

Don't do things that you are uncomfortable with, that embarrass you, or that could get you in trouble, just to make other people like you or laugh.

Do not make fun of others or bully them.

Agree or Disagree?

Read each sentence. Color the thumb to tell if you agree, disagree, or are not sure.

It is important to treat your classmates with respect, even when you are not in the classroom.

Kids should try to stand up for other kids who are being mistreated at school.

It's not very important to have friends at school.

It is not my responsibility to have healthy habits, like covering my mouth when I cough or washing my hands.

It's not my job to help my classmates, even if I can see that they need help.

It's important that I'm treated fairly in class, and it's important that other people are treated fairly, too.

Choices at School

Kids have to make a lot of choices at school. Some choices are not easy to make. It is not always easy to know what is the right thing to do. And sometimes, even if you know what is right, it is not always easy to do the right thing.

Read the story. Then answer the questions.

Mrs. Khoulani told the class to find a spot at a science lab station while she gathered materials. Darius went to the same station as Madison, and then Carlos and Eli joined them. Latoya chose a different station, along with Archie, followed by Jenny, Michael, and Bree. Suddenly there was a lot of giggling. Carlos got up and went to Latoya's station. There was more giggling as Michael, who was on his way to Madison's station, turned around and went to a third lab station. Then Maria studied the groups for a moment. Even though she and Madison are best friends, she went to Michael's station. Madison frowned at her small group and also moved to Michael's station. The rest of the class went to the last station or crowded into the other stations—except Eli's.

Eventually, it was just Darius at the same station as Eli. Unlike the other kids, Darius was kind of bothered by what he was seeing, and he felt bad for Eli. But he could feel his own face get hot, and he felt nervous. He was aware that the giggling was still happening. So what did Darius do? He got up with a smile and moved across the room to get as far away from Eli as he could, and he joined in with the giggling.

When the teacher faced the class to start the lab lesson, she told her students to make the groups more even. Some kids moved with a low groan, and Eli did end up working with other kids. The teacher had not noticed what had happened minutes earlier.

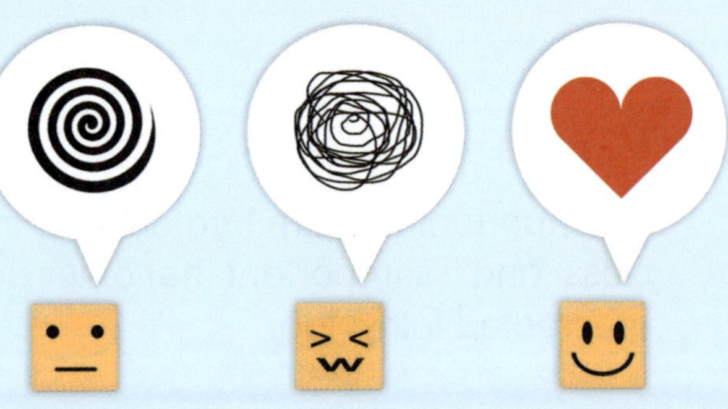

Sometimes it's easy to know what the right thing to do is, and sometimes it's not easy. Do you think Darius knew what the right thing to do was?

◯ yes ◯ no

What do you think Darius should have done? Do you think Darius did the right thing? Explain.

____

____

Why do you think Darius did what he did?

____

____

Do you think you might have done the same thing Darius did? Draw to show what you would have done. Draw what you imagine Eli's face looked like as the groups formed.

Joining In

Every recess, you probably get free time inside or outdoors. You might see a group of students from your class playing a game or talking together. How could you ask to join in?

Read the situations in the center ovals. Then read and write in the boxes to brainstorm different ways you can ask to join in.

If I see one of my friends playing on the field, I could…

If I do not see anyone I know on the field, I could…

You see a group of kids your age kicking around a soccer ball. You love to play soccer, too! The group is making teams so they can play a game together. **How can you ask to join in?**

I could ask them a question that starts with "Can I…"

I could ask them a question that starts with "Are you looking for…"

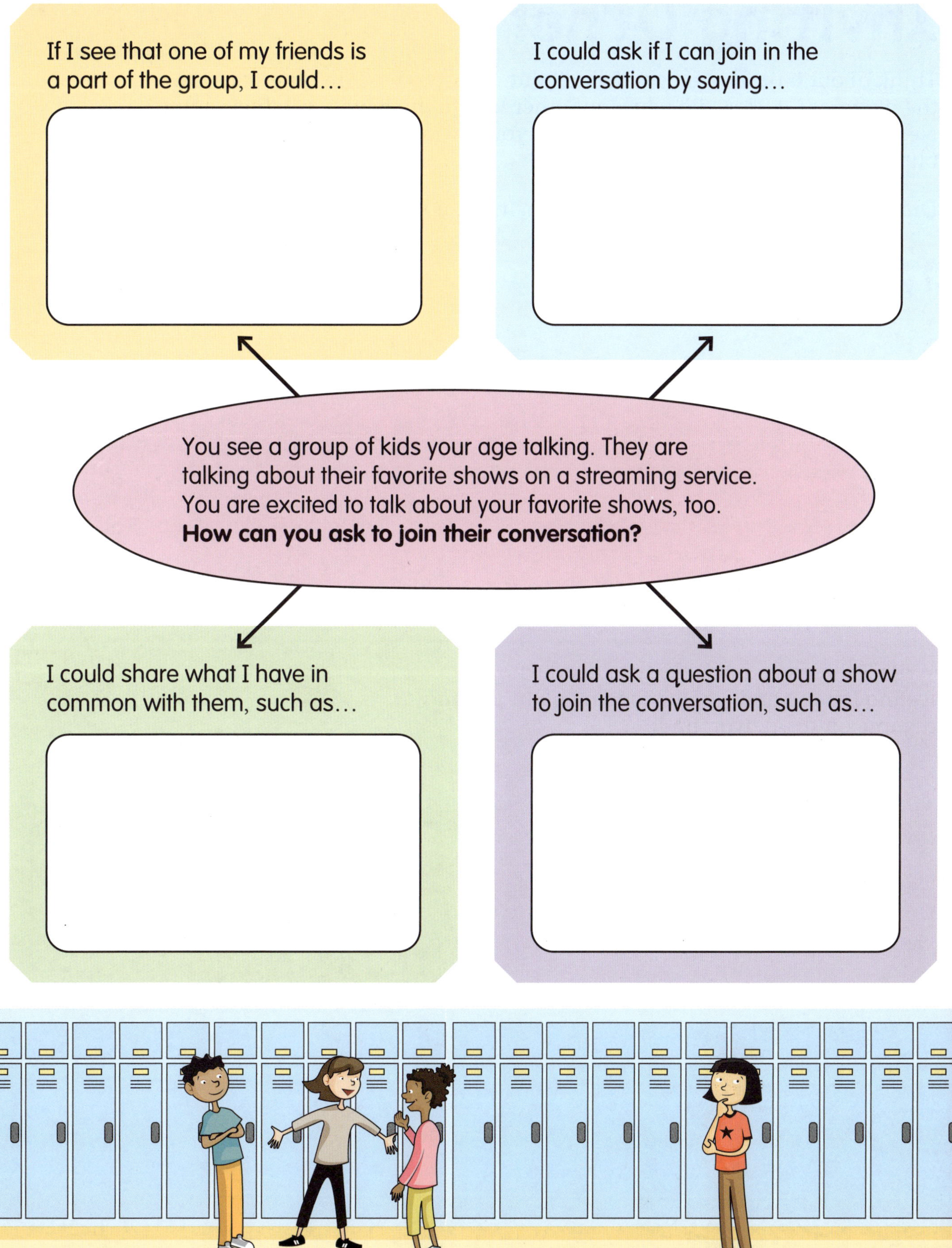
If I see that one of my friends is a part of the group, I could...
I could ask if I can join in the conversation by saying...
You see a group of kids your age talking. They are talking about their favorite shows on a streaming service. You are excited to talk about your favorite shows, too.
How can you ask to join their conversation?
I could share what I have in common with them, such as...
I could ask a question about a show to join the conversation, such as...

Inviting Others

Think about a time when you felt left out or wanted to join other kids on the playground. How did you want other kids to invite you into their game? Next, think about what you could do if you saw a kid who was feeling left out and wanted to join your game.

Draw to show one thing you could do to invite a kid into your game.

Write 2 things you would say to a kid who was feeling left out and wanted to join you in playing a game on the playground.

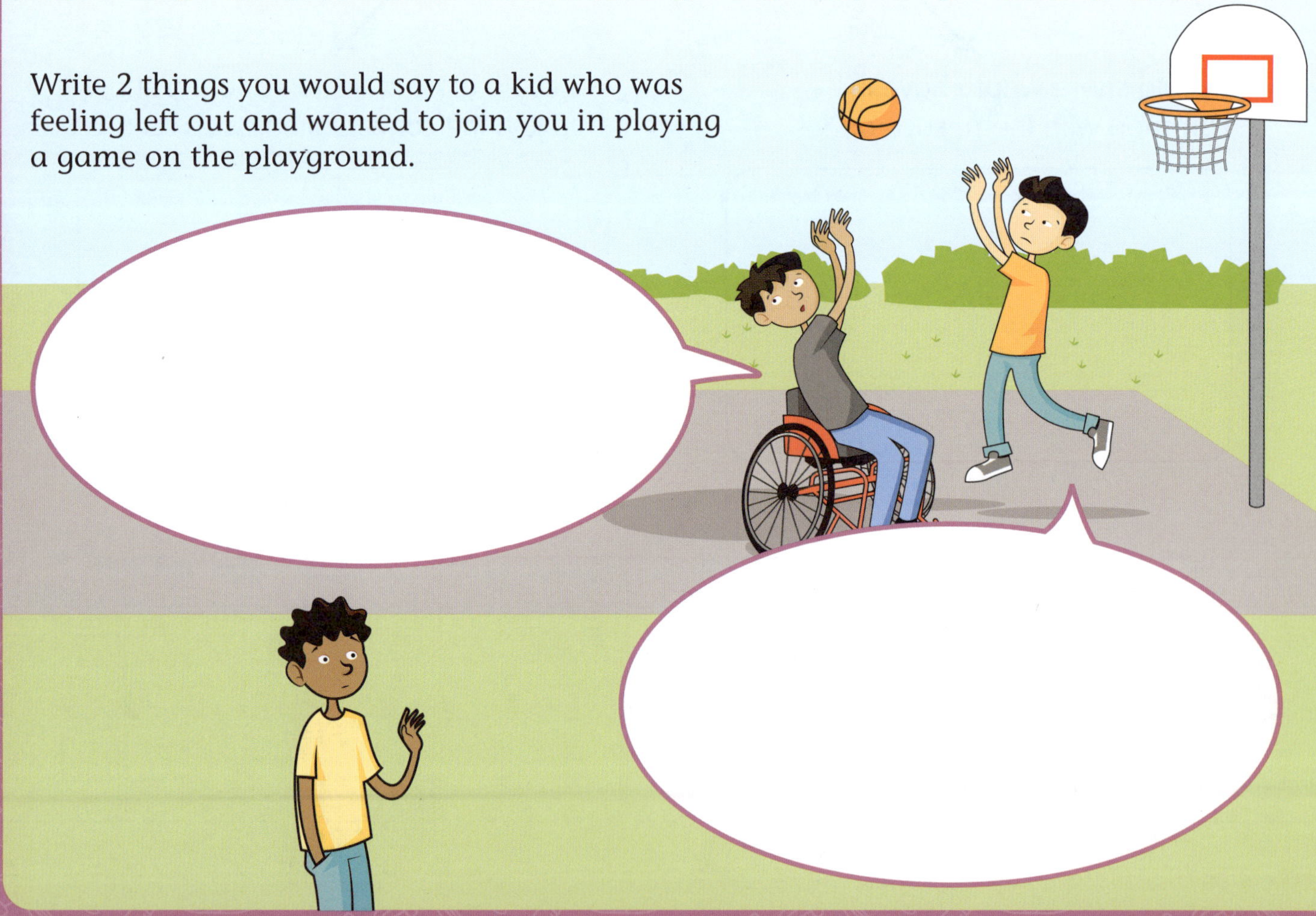

I Can Adjust

Think about the things you usually do at recess. Do you usually spend recess alone? Do you usually spend recess with friends? Do you do the same activity every day? There might be days when you can't do what you usually do. You can adjust, or you can do something different once in a while.

Draw to show one thing you do or could do alone at recess.

Draw to show one thing you could do with other kids at recess that you don't usually do.

Feelings Word Cloud

Lots of things can happen at recess. Sometimes kids play. Sometimes kids just talk. And sometimes kids are alone. There are times when kids play nicely and times they don't. Think about all the feelings you have ever had at recess. All feelings are okay, and no feelings are wrong.

Make a word cloud to show all the feelings you have when you're at school at recess.

What You Need

- page 55
- sheet of light-colored construction paper
- scissors
- markers or crayons
- glue or tape
- materials to decorate, such as glitter, paint, stickers, stamps, cotton balls, foil, or beads

What You Do

1. Read the feeling words on page 55. You can cut out any of the words to put on your word cloud. You can also write your own words to put on the word cloud.
2. Draw a big cloud on the construction paper. Glue and write words inside the cloud you drew.
3. Decorate the word cloud.
4. Show the word cloud to family or friends, and talk about when or why you think you have had these feelings.

SERIOUS

SILLY

ANXIOUS

ANGRY

CHILL

DISAPPOINTED

LONELY

JEALOUS

UPBEAT

EXCITED

BUSY

DOWN

CURIOUS

HAPPY

CHEERFUL

NICE

ENERGETIC

SAD

BORED

NERVOUS

ANNOYED

PROTECTIVE

MEAN

TIRED

Journal Your Feelings

Everyone has big feelings sometimes, such as fear, anger, and loneliness. When you feel a big feeling, it can help to write about it. You can write about what you are feeling, along with some ideas to help you move forward.

Read the journal questions. Choose one to write about and answer.

Journal questions:

1. Write about a time when you felt afraid to ask someone to play with you at school. What helped you deal with your fear?
2. Write about a time when you felt angry with someone at school or during recess. How did you let the other person know how you were feeling?
3. Write about a time when you felt lonely at the school playground. How did you find a way to reach out to someone else when you felt lonely? Or did someone reach out to you?

Measure the Problem

You might face conflict or problems on the playground. Someone may say something mean to you, or maybe someone isn't taking turns. Some problems are smaller than other problems. Knowing a problem's size can help you decide what to do about it.

Read about different sizes of problems. This is just one way that you might choose to look at problems that can come up at school.

MINI PROBLEM EXAMPLE:
Someone mispronounces your name by accident. You feel hurt, but the person says he or she is sorry.

SAMPLE SOLUTION:
You might choose to let go of this kind of problem. You can tell the person how to say your name and then keep playing.

MEDIUM PROBLEM EXAMPLE:
Your friends did not invite you to play tag with them.

SAMPLE SOLUTION:
You might want to talk to a friend or a family member about this kind of problem. You can let your friends know that you felt hurt and wish they had asked you to play.

BIG PROBLEM EXAMPLE:
You see someone push your friend on the playground. Your friend falls and gets hurt.

SAMPLE SOLUTION:
You might want to get help from an adult to solve this kind of problem. You find an adult and take him or her to your friend who is hurt.

Are you facing a mini, medium, or big problem on the playground?

Read the decision tree below to learn about some choices you can make when you have a problem at school.

What "size" is this problem?

START

Will this problem still bother me later today?

- Yes, it will.
  - Is someone hurt or at risk? Does someone need help from an adult?
    - Yes. → **Big Problem**
    - No, I don't think so.
      - Have you tried talking to the person you are having a problem with?
        - Yes, many times. → **Big Problem**
        - Not yet. → **Medium Problem**
- No, it will not even matter to me in an hour or two. → **Mini Problem**

Mini Problem

This is likely a mini problem. You might choose to let go or ignore this problem.

Big Problem

This might be a big problem. You might want to get help from an adult to help you solve this problem.

Medium Problem

This may be a medium problem. You could try talking to the other person first.

My Conflict Choices

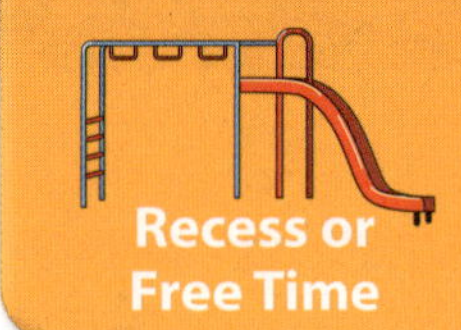

You might face conflict or problems when spending time with other people at school. When we face conflict, we have choices for how to respond. Think about different choices you can make when you have a problem at school.

You will use cards to have a conversation and brainstorm ideas about ways to solve conflicts at school.

Conflict Card #3
You want to play hopscotch, but someone else is already playing it. You wait your turn, but the other person keeps playing and playing ev... fter he wins. What choices ... make?

Conflict Card #1
Your friend Jemma asks you to play tag with some other students. But you do not like to play tag and would rather use chalk to draw pictures on the sidewalk. What choices can you make?

Conflict Card #5
Your friend Carlos wants to play with you. But you have not seen your friend Anna all summer and want to play with her instead. What choices can you make?

What You Need

- page 61
- scissors
- a friend or parent

What You Do

1. Cut out the cards on page 61. Shuffle the orange conflict cards and put them facedown. Put the other three blue cards faceup.
2. Choose a conflict card and read it aloud. Then choose one of the other three cards and follow the directions. Repeat for the other two cards until you have explained all three options to end the conflict.
3. Ask your friend or parent if he or she agrees with your "win-win" solution to the conflict. Ask why or why not.
4. Next, it's the other person's turn to choose a card and read it aloud. This person follows step 2 above. Then you can tell if you agree with this person's idea for a "win-win" solution to the conflict.
5. Keep going until you have gone through all of the cards!

Conflict Card #1

Your friend Jemma asks you to play tag with some other students. But you do not like to play tag and would rather use chalk to draw pictures on the sidewalk. What choices can you make?

Conflict Card #2

Your friend Jamal is on the playground with another friend. You say "hello!" to him, but he turns his head, and it seems like he's ignoring you. You feel hurt. What choices can you make?

Conflict Card #3

You want to play hopscotch, but someone else is already playing it. You wait your turn, but the other person keeps playing and playing even after he wins. What choices can you make?

Conflict Card #4

You are playing tag with a group of friends. You overhear someone say that you run really slowly. You feel upset. What choices can you make?

Conflict Card #5

Your friend Carlos wants to play with you. But you have not seen your friend Anna all summer and want to play with her instead. What choices can you make?

Conflict Card #6

You and a group of friends want to play spikeball. But there are five of you, and only four people can play spikeball at a time. What choices can you make?

Lose-Lose

Tell about a lose-lose end to the conflict where both people leave the conflict unhappy.

Win-Lose

Tell about a win-lose end to the conflict where one person leaves the conflict happy and the other person leaves the conflict unhappy.

Win-Win

Tell about a win-win end to the conflict where both people leave the conflict feeling heard and happy.

Calming Tools at School

My Feelings About Lunch

People have different eating habits, and they may do things differently when they eat. It is okay to have certain things that you like or dislike about meal times. When you are eating with other people, they can try to be accepting of your eating habits, and you can try to be accepting of their eating habits, too.

Read about the habits that some people have at lunch time. Write a √ in the speech bubble to tell if the eating habit describes you sometimes.

I like to talk a lot at lunchtime. Sometimes I talk so much that I almost don't have enough time to eat all my food!

I don't like to talk much when I'm eating.

I like to eat most foods with my hands. That's how I eat a lot of foods at home. It's something we do in my family's culture.

I don't like to eat any foods with my hands.

I don't like to smell other people's foods.

I like to see and smell what other people are eating for lunch.

Write 2 things that describe you and how you feel when you eat lunch at school.

Lunch Rules at School

Most schools have some lunchtime rules. Rules can help make lunchtime clean and healthy for students. Rules can also help lunch go smoothly so that it begins and ends on time and you can continue doing other things at school.

Read each school lunchtime rule. Then draw a picture to show what it would look like if that rule was **not** followed by students.

Rule: Throw away your garbage after you eat.

Rule: Sit at the lunch table when you are eating.

Rule: Stand in line and wait your turn to buy lunch.

Rule: Eat only your own food.

Eating Lunch Alone

Some people like to eat lunch with their friends or classmates. Some people might like to eat lunch alone or not talk that much when they eat lunch. Everyone's feelings at lunch are okay. What if you see someone eating alone and you are not sure if he or she wants to be eating alone?

Imagine that you see a kid in the school cafeteria eating alone, day after day. Write things in the circles that you could say to that person. Read the example.

Things I could say to the kid eating alone:

I noticed that you eat alone some days. Do you want to be eating alone, or would you rather eat with other people?

Snack Bags

Decorate snack bags for you and a friend to use for a school snack. You can show things that you and your friend like on the snack bags.

What You Need

- page 69
- 2 paper bags
- scissors
- tape or glue
- materials to decorate
- snacks to put in the bags

What You Do

1. Choose a friend whom you want to make a snack bag for. You will make snack bags for you and your friend.
2. Decorate each bag. Write your name on your bag, and write your friend's name on your friend's bag. You can use the pictures and words on page 69 to decorate your bags.
3. After you have finished decorating the snack bags, you may need to let them dry.
4. Then fill the snack bags with snacks that you and your friend like.
5. Bring the snack bags to school and give one to your friend!

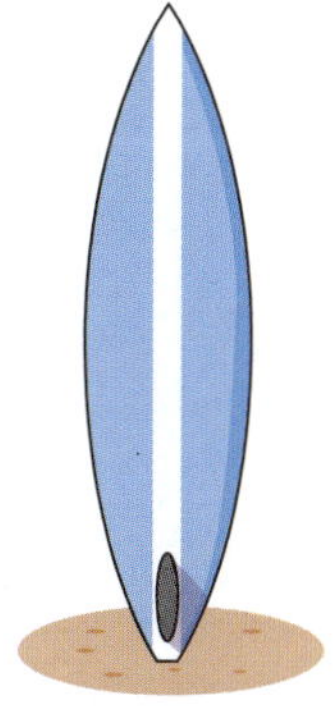

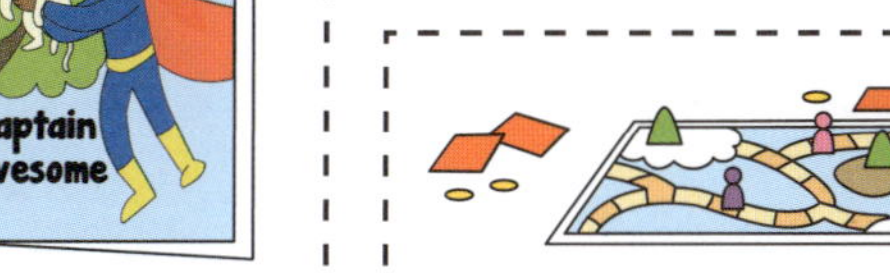

GAMES

PETS

Sleepovers

Going Places

There are many things to think about when you go places.

- ☆ You can think about whether you want to say hi and how to greet people.
- ☆ You can think about how the people you see are the same and different.
- ☆ You can think about things you want to do or don't want to do.
- ☆ You can think about how to treat people with respect everywhere you go.

You probably go to many different places. There are many different people you see when you go places. You can try to make respectful choices to be considerate of others. You can also make choices to help yourself when you go places.

Places I Go

People go to a lot of different places. Different places have different rules. You may choose to act a certain way in one place and differently in another place, and that is okay.

Read the places. Draw a ☆ in the ☐ to show if it's a place you go sometimes. Then write 2 other places you go at the bottom of the page.

- ☐ grocery store
- ☐ clothing store
- ☐ ballpark or stadium
- ☐ public transportation, such as a bus or train
- ☐ restaurants
- ☐ park
- ☐ doctor's office
- ☐ haircut shop
- ☐ bowling alley

Remove and display this chart where you can see it.

How to Greet People

Making Assumptions

You see many people when you go places. Every person looks different, feels differently, and thinks differently. It is important to not make assumptions about people. An assumption is a guess that you believe is true about someone. But an assumption is not a fact; it's only a guess. Sometimes when people assume or make assumptions about a person, it affects how they treat that person.

Read each assumption below.
Then write what you would think instead.

A person needs your help if he or she has a disability.

Instead, I think ______________________________.

You can tell what a person's personality is like based on how that person looks.

Instead, I think ______________________________.

All disabilities are visible or are noticeable.

Instead, I think ______________________________.

It is okay to touch or feed another person's pet or service animal.

Instead, I think ______________________________.

You can tell that someone is from a certain country or speaks a certain language because of how he or she looks.

Instead, I think ______________________________.

People Are Different

You see many people when you go places. Every person looks different and is different in many ways. You may see a person who is not like anyone you have ever seen before. It is okay to observe how other people are different from you and the same as you.

Read the descriptions of some people. Trace the stars with descriptions that match with someone you have seen before.

Some people . . .

- use a wheelchair
- have red hair
- have freckles
- are shorter than you
- have curly hair
- are taller than you
- wear a head scarf

wear glasses

have brown eyes

have darker skin than you

have lighter skin than you

have only one arm or only one leg

have blue eyes

Write 3 more ways that people can be different from you.

Different Is Cool

The world would not be as interesting to see if there were only one kind of line. Just like there are many different kinds of lines, there are many different kinds of people. Draw a picture that uses many different kinds of lines to show how being different is cool.

What You Need

- page 79
- markers or colored pencils

What You Do

1. Think about the different kinds of lines there are.

straight

zigzag

wavy

looped

curly

scalloped

2. Draw a different kind of line in each box on the next page. Use different colors.
3. After you finish, remove your picture from the book, cut it out, and hang it where you can see it. Use it to remind yourself that being different is cool!

Space Intruder or Respecter?

You might go to a store or other public place using a car or bus. It's important to respect other people's personal space when you are in a car or on a bus. Read about how people treat personal space. Then answer the questions.

Space intruders...	Space respecters...
• stand or sit an inch or less away from family and friends • stand or sit a foot or less away from strangers • do not notice if someone beside them looks uncomfortable	• keep an arm's length of space between themselves and their family and friends • keep two arms' length between themselves and strangers • notice if someone beside them looks uncomfortable

Do you think the young person in the picture is a space intruder or space respecter? Tell why.

____

____

____

Do you think the young person in the picture is a space intruder or space respecter? Tell why.

____

____

____

Volume Up or Down?

We use different volume levels in different public spaces. One way you can figure out the "voice volume" of any public space is to listen to other people around you. What is the volume of their voice?

Think about different public spaces and their "voice volume levels." Cut out the volume level descriptions and examples on page 83. Glue them where you think they go in the chart below.

	Volume Description	Volume Example
LOW		
HIGH		

Example: I would use this voice volume while playing with my friends outside at the park.	**Voice Volume 3:** I speak at a natural volume with a small group of people. This is my inside voice.
Example: I would use this voice volume to speak to my friend beside me at the movie theatre.	**Example:** I would use this voice volume in the "silent" section at my library.
Example: I would use this voice volume when talking with my parents at the grocery store.	**Voice Volume 2:** I whisper very quietly to one person. Only that person can hear what I say.
Voice Volume 4: I yell when I am feeling excited and playing with others. This is my outside voice.	**Voice Volume 5:** I scream for help because there is an emergency.
Voice Volume 1: I am silent and do not speak at all.	**Example:** I would only use this voice volume if someone were in danger or at risk.

Healthy When I Go Places

When you go places, you can do things that help you stay healthy and safe and that help keep other people healthy, too.

Write a √ next to things you do to help keep yourself and others healthy.

- ☐ I wash my hands in the restroom.
- ☐ I use a tissue to wipe my nose instead of using my hands.
- ☐ I do not touch other people's food or drink without asking.
- ☐ I keep my distance from people when I am sick.
- ☐ I follow health rules that are posted.

Draw one more thing you do to keep yourself and others healthy.

Sick at the Mall

Read the story. Write phrases from the box to finish the story.

Your mom told you to take some
covering your sneeze, Sage
your sneeze!

Trudaci loved going to the mall with his friends. They always went to see what was new at the Games Depot and hang out at the food court. Sage and Sean were getting a ride to the mall together. Trudaci met his friends at the entrance to the mall. He noticed that Sean did not look well. "Hey, Sean, are you feeling okay?" he asked.

"Yeah, I'm okay," said Sean as he sneezed all over them. "I'm just a little under the weather."

"Dude, you should have stayed home if you are sick! And cover ______________________________" said Trudaci.

"Sorry, Tru. I didn't want to miss the new game releases," said Sean.

Suddenly, Sage turned his body away and threw his elbow up to his face. "Achoo!" Sage sneezed. Then he took a tissue out of his pocket to blow his nose.

"Thanks for ______________________________," said Trudaci.

"Do you have any more tissues, Sage?" asked Sean as he coughed.

"______________________________," said Sage, "but I'll give you my last clean one." Sage grabbed hand sanitizer out of his pocket and cleaned his hands before handing Sean a clean tissue.

Trudaci looked at both of his friends and knew they should not be going to the mall. Their coughing and sneezing would spread too many germs. "Hey guys, why don't we meet here next week when you are feeling better? I don't want to get what you have," said Trudaci.

"Yeah, I'm not feeling great," said Sage. "I'll see if my mom can pick us up now."

Talk with Your Family

Restaurant Expectations

There are a lot of things to think about when you go to a restaurant. Most restaurants have some rules. There are some behaviors that you might want to do and some that you might not want to do at a restaurant. Your comfort and happiness at a restaurant are important. It is also important to consider the comfort and happiness of other people at the restaurant.

Read the questions below with your parents. Talk about the answers.

- Is it okay to talk loudly at a restaurant?
- Do I need to put my napkin on my lap at a restaurant?
- Can I reach across the table at a restaurant?
- Can I order my own food at a restaurant?
- When I'm done eating, is it okay for me to get up and walk around?
- Can I go to the restaurant bathroom on my own?
- Is it okay to text or talk on the phone at a restaurant?
- Is it okay to run in a restaurant?
- Is it okay for me to help the server?

What to Say at a Restaurant

When you go to a restaurant, a server will help you. Try to think about servers' feelings and how to treat them with respect.

When you go to a restaurant, you might have to order food for yourself. Read the examples of what you could say. Then write one more thing you could say.

Examples:

Can I please have the ______________________?

I would like ______________________, please.

I'll have the same thing, please.

One more thing I could say:

When you go to a restaurant, you might have to talk after the server brings you food. Read the examples of what you could say. Then write one more thing you could say.

Examples:

Thank you!

Sorry, but my order isn't exactly right.

This looks really good.

One more thing I could say:

How Do You Handle It?

Sometimes something uncomfortable can happen at a restaurant and you have to decide how to handle it.

Read about the different situations. Write to tell how you would handle each situation.

You are really looking forward to having a scoop of your favorite ice cream. Sonja is a server. She brings you the wrong flavor of ice cream by mistake. How do you handle it?

It is your birthday and your parents are taking you and your friends out for breakfast. You are really hungry. When your pancakes get to the table, you accidentally knock your plate to the floor. How do you handle it?

You go to a restaurant with your friend's family. You have never been there before, and you don't see any foods on the menu that you like. How do you handle it?

Treating Servers with Respect

Many situations occur in restaurants. There are respectful ways to handle any situation. Read about the situations below. Are the characters treating their servers with respect? Color the emojis to rate the behavior of the characters.

☆ = not respectful ☆☆☆ = somewhat respectful  ☆☆☆☆☆ = very respectful

Situation 1

Your rating:

Situation 2

Your rating:

How Do Other Diners Feel?

When you are eating at a restaurant, it is important that you feel comfortable. It is also important that other people feel comfortable, too. There are some things people can do to help themselves and other people feel comfortable at a restaurant.

Read the sentences about things that make some people feel comfortable or uncomfortable. In each box, write to tell why you think these things make people feel that way.

Comfortable

Sit at the table with your chair scooted in.

Speak politely and not too loudly.

Uncomfortable

Stand in the way of people who are working.

Play with your food and make a mess on the table and floor.

Restaurant Bingo

There are many fun experiences you can have when you eat at a restaurant.

Read the squares. Choose a square to do. After you do it, color the square. When you have colored all the squares, yell BINGO!

BINGO		
Order your food yourself.	Ask a question about something on the menu.	Hold the door open for someone leaving or entering the restaurant.
Go to a restaurant that has entertainment.	Try a food you have never had before.	Ask your parents if you can choose a restaurant to go to.
Recommend a food that you like to your family or a friend.	Put your napkin in your lap and use it during your meal.	Ask a friend if he or she can recommend a restaurant he or she likes.
Use an eating tool you have never used before.	Ask your parents if they would like you to make a reservation.	Recommend a restaurant you like to one of your friends.

How Do You Feel?

It can take time and practice to feel comfortable and confident shopping at a store.

Think about the stores you have been to. Think about what you are comfortable or not comfortable doing. Read each scenario below and color the circle with the number that tells how you feel about it.

(1) I don't like to do it.
(2) I will do it, but I feel uncomfortable.
(3) I don't feel strongly either way.
(4) I like to do it.

asking a person who works in a store a question

(1) (2) (3) (4)

answering a question that another shopper asks you

(1) (2) (3) (4)

picking up things that accidentally fell to the floor

(1) (2) (3) (4)

asking a person who works at the store where the restroom is

(1) (2) (3) (4)

asking the clerk at the cash register about your purchase, such as, "Excuse me, wasn't this shirt on sale?"

(1) (2) (3) (4)

Things That Happen at the Store

Draw a picture of something that you think would be awkward or embarrassing if it happened to you at the store. Write a sentence to tell about it.

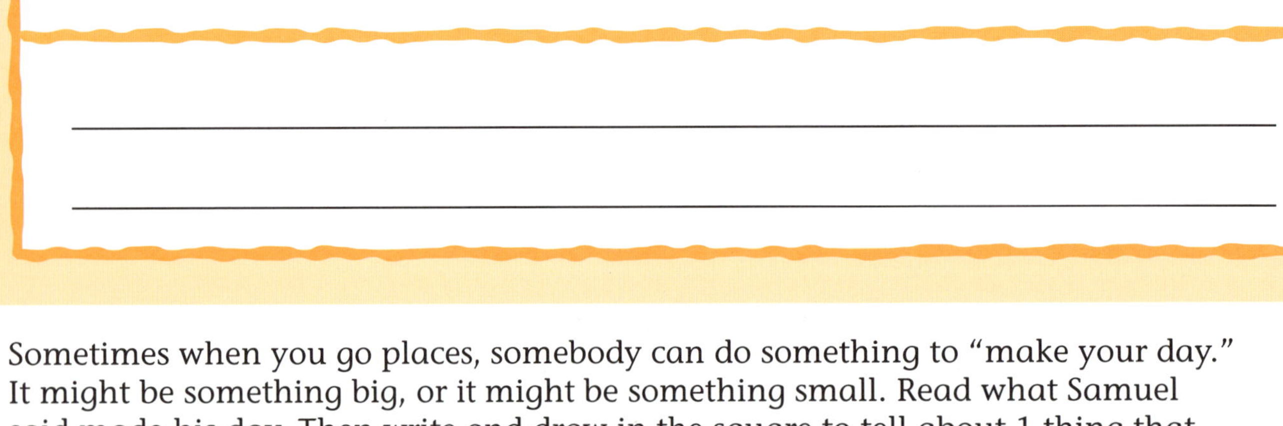

Sometimes when you go places, somebody can do something to "make your day." It might be something big, or it might be something small. Read what Samuel said made his day. Then write and draw in the square to tell about 1 thing that could make your day.

The man in front of me in line won a free candy bar as a prize for being the 100th customer that day. He smiled and gave it to me!

Talk with Your Family

What Is Okay at the Store?

There are a lot of things that people do at home that they do not do when they go places such as stores. Sometimes this is because they feel more comfortable doing some things in private. Sometimes it's because stores have rules. When you go to a store, it's important to think about your own comfort but also to be considerate of other people.

Read the questions below with your parents.
Talk about the answers.

Is it okay if I ask the people who work at the store questions?

Is it okay if I do things that I do at home at the store, such as take my shoes off, sit on the floor, or eat snacks?

Is it okay if I pick up things in other people's shopping carts?

Is it okay if I make a mess at the store and leave it for store workers to clean up?

Behavior at a Store

It is important to have positive behavior when you go shopping at a store. Your behavior affects the people around you. And the behavior of the people at the store affects you.

Read the stories and the descriptions on page 97. Then cut them out. Glue to match a story to a description that tells about the main character, or write a description of your own on the blank green square.

glue	glue
glue	glue
glue	glue
glue	glue
glue	glue

Jeff was standing in line and waiting his turn to pay for his items. He made sure not to stand too close to the person in front of him. He also made sure he had enough money to pay for everything that he wanted to buy.

Amree was in a hurry to bring snacks to her friend's house. As Amree waited in line to pay for the snacks, she crowded the person in front of her. Then the person asked the clerk a question. Amree sighed loudly and rolled her eyes as she said, "I'm in a hurry!"

Anthony loves shopping for shoes. He asked the clerk to bring him many pairs to try on. After he tried on the shoes, he threw the ones he did not want onto the floor. Then he kicked the boxes out of the way as he walked to the register with the pair he wanted to buy.

Julius was looking at the ice cream flavors when a kid ran down the aisle yelling loudly. The kid opened freezer door and hopped onto the ledge as he shouted, "I'm hungry!" Julius did not think this was safe behavior. He decided to go into another aisle.

Minh noticed the lady next to her trying to get a box off of the top shelf. The box was hard for the lady to reach, but Minh could reach it easily. Minh asked the lady, "Excuse me, would you like some help getting that box?"

considerate	not considerate	responsible
not respectful	helpful	

Signs You Like

What signs would you like to see when you go into a store? Color them.

Helpful Videos

Did you know that many people learn about social skills by watching videos? Videos can show choices that people can make and how some choices are helpful while other choices are not as helpful. You can make your own videos about how to act in stores. One video can show choices that are helpful or that can make a situation better. The other video can show choices that are not helpful or that can make a situation worse. Maybe your videos will help someone learn more about social skills!

What You Need

- pages 101 and 102
- scissors
- a smartphone or video device
- any materials or props you want to use, such as hats, clothes, a table, etc.
- 2 people to help make the video: 1 person to act in the video with you and 1 person to record it

What You Do

1. Cut out the scripts on pages 101 and 102. The Helpful Video Script is on one side and the Not Helpful Video Script is on the other side. Read both scripts and think about how you will act to show both situations.
2. Decide which person will act as the customer and which person will act as the employee in the video. Also decide who will record the video.
3. Record the "Not Helpful" video first using the script. Use any materials or props you want in the video.
4. Next, record the "Helpful" video using the script.
5. After you have finished recording the videos, watch them. Then decide if you would like to show your videos to other people.

Helpful Video Script

(Scene: Customer in store is holding a clothing item and trying to get a nearby employee's attention.)

Customer: *(waves)* Hi there! Sorry to bother you, but I've been waiting a long time. Is there someone who can help me buy this?

Employee: *(smiles)* Sorry about the wait. We are a bit busy today. How can I help?

Customer: I have a question about this item. Do you know if it was made locally?

Employee: *(has an unsure facial expression)* I am not sure about that.

Customer: Is there a way you could find out?

Employee: I am the only person working here now. Would you be willing to leave your phone number, and I can call you later after I find out the answer to your question?

Customer: Sure! I'd like that.

Employee: Okay, I will give you a call later today.

Customer: Great! Even though you couldn't answer my question right away, I appreciate you looking into it and that you are trying to help me.

Helpful Video Script

(Scene: Customer in store is holding a clothing item and trying to get a nearby employee's attention.)

Customer: *(waves)* Hi there! Sorry to bother you, but I've been waiting a long time. Is there someone who can help me buy this?

Employee: *(smiles)* Sorry about the wait. We are a bit busy today. How can I help?

Customer: I have a question about this item. Do you know if it was made locally?

Employee: *(has an unsure facial expression)* I am not sure about that.

Customer: Is there a way you could find out?

Employee: I am the only person working here now. Would you be willing to leave your phone number, and I can call you later after I find out the answer to your question?

Customer: Sure! I'd like that.

Employee: Okay, I will give you a call later today.

Customer: Great! Even though you couldn't answer my question right away, I appreciate you looking into it and that you are trying to help me.

Not Helpful Video Script

(Scene: Customer in store is holding a clothing item and trying to get a nearby employee's attention.)

Customer: *(coughs loudly, stomps, sighs loudly)*

Employee: *(looks over at customer, rolls eyes, and then looks away)*

Customer: Hey! Hey you there! Do you have any idea how long I have been waiting to get some help? Are you going to help me or are you going to keep ignoring me?

Employee: *(has a negative tone of voice)* Okay, what do you want?

Customer: Well, I might want to buy this. I have a question first. Did your store buy this from a local clothing maker?

Employee: I'm not sure about that.

Customer: You mean you work here but you can't even answer a basic question? I want to speak to a manager about your poor customer service.

Employee: Are you going to buy this or what?

Customer: *(throws item on the counter)* No way! I'm leaving, and I'm never coming back.

Not Helpful Video Script

(Scene: Customer in store is holding a clothing item and trying to get a nearby employee's attention.)

Customer: *(coughs loudly, stomps, sighs loudly)*

Employee: *(looks over at customer, rolls eyes, and then looks away)*

Customer: Hey! Hey you there! Do you have any idea how long I have been waiting to get some help? Are you going to help me or are you going to keep ignoring me?

Employee: *(has a negative tone of voice)* Okay, what do you want?

Customer: Well, I might want to buy this. I have a question first. Did your store buy this from a local clothing maker?

Employee: I'm not sure about that.

Customer: You mean you work here but you can't even answer a basic question? I want to speak to a manager about your poor customer service.

Employee: Are you going to buy this or what?

Customer: *(throws item on the counter)* No way! I'm leaving, and I'm never coming back.

Being Online

You can talk to friends and do other things online. There are things to think about when you go online.

- ☆ Typing something is different from saying something to someone in person.
- ☆ You can choose to be kind and respectful online, just like when you are offline.
- ☆ You can control what you post online.
- ☆ You can make choices when you are online.

Sometimes it can be hard to know what the right choices are when you are online. It can help if you think about your choices carefully and talk to your family about them.

Page 104

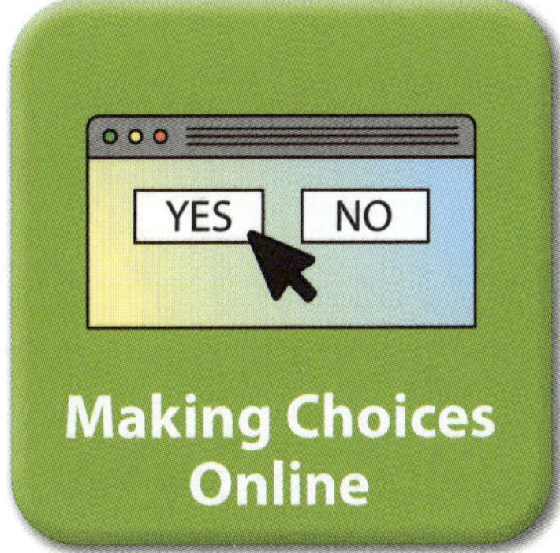

Page 112

Digital-Respect Checklist

Sometimes you might send messages or videos to someone online. Before you click "send" or "share," it can help to go through a digital-respect checklist.

Read the checklist. Write an **X** next to each item you agree with. Then write 2 items of your own.

Digital-Respect Checklist

Before I send or share a digital message or video, I check these things:

- ☐ I have thought about how someone might feel when he or she receives this message.
- ☐ I am sharing information that is honest and kind.
- ☐ I am sending or sharing a message or video with people I trust. I also make sure that strangers will not see this message.
- ☐ If there are other people in my message or video, I have their permission to send or share the message or video.
- ☐ I have thought about whether I will still be happy that I sent this message or video a year from now.
- ☐ If I have any fears or doubts about the message or video, I check in with my parent or another adult first before I click Send.
- ☐ Write your own: ____________________
- ☐ Write your own: ____________________

Be a "Tone" Detective!

Every digital message has a "tone of voice." Tone helps you understand the attitude or personality of the person sending the message. We often use a different "tone" when we send messages to different people.

You can be a "tone" detective when you read or send a message! Read the messages below for each tone. Circle or highlight the clues that tell you about the tone of the message.

#1: THE CASUAL OR FRIENDLY TONE

Nah, I can't make it tonight.

Hey buddy! How's it going?

Wow, I love your shirt! It's so cute and colorful.

You might use this tone with…

- your friends
- your close family, like your parents or siblings
- people who know you well

Aw, thanks, you're the best!

#2: THE FORMAL OR RESPECTFUL TONE

Dear Ms. Ling,
May I ask you a question?

Thank you for thinking of me.

Hello. My name is Julie Hanks.

Respectfully,
Kareem

You might use this tone with…

- your teacher
- some family members, such as your grandparents
- people you do not know very well

Can you please resend it?

Message Misunderstandings

Read the story. Then answer the questions on the next page.

"I'm busy, can't make it," read the text message. Axel looked at the text in disbelief. It was Saturday afternoon, and Sam was supposed to come to Axel's house to play board games. But instead of coming over, she had sent a short text to Axel.

Most of the time, Sam wrote long paragraphs and almost always included emojis in her texts, but this time she didn't. Axel rubbed his forehead. Had he done something wrong? Or did Sam not want to be friends anymore? Axel's thoughts began to swirl in a spiral. Sam didn't text him as often anymore… and she had started hanging out with Aisha more and more…

As Axel's thoughts spun around, he got more and more irritated. Finally, he decided to send Sam a text to let her know she wasn't welcome at his house anymore. "You're clearly too busy to be friends with me," Axel began texting, "so why don't we just stop hanging out." Axel was about to hit Send when his dad walked in.

"What's going on, Axel?" his dad said. "You look a bit upset."

Axel told his dad about the text message from Sam. His dad nodded and then put his arm around Axel. "It makes sense you're feeling uncertain about your friendship with Sam. But I just heard from her mom. Sam's aunt is in the hospital. Maybe that's why she sent you a short text—she's feeling anxious about her aunt."

"Oh," Axel said, feeling his face get red. He quickly deleted his text. "I feel kind of bad now."

"Well, just keep in mind that text messages are hard to read sometimes. We can only see the words, and we don't always know the entire story behind the words. If you are ever confused or upset about a message, it usually helps to ask your friend in person. That way, you can see the person's body language and hear the tone of his or her voice."

Later that day, Axel sent Sam a message telling her he was thinking of her and her aunt. Sam sent back a "❤️" in response.

Axel received a message from Sam that was short.
Would you have felt confused and hurt like Axel? Tell why or why not.

Tell about a time when you misunderstood a written message from someone else.

If you received a message from someone and felt confused or upset, what would you do next? Draw or write your answer.

To Emoji or Not?

Some people like to use emojis in their e-mails or text messages. Emojis are icons or tiny pictures you can send in your message. Emojis are also a way to tell someone what you feel or think.

Answer the questions.

Do you like to add emojis to your e-mails or texts? Tell why or why not.

____

____

____

What do different emojis mean to you? Look at the emojis below. Write 1 or 2 words to describe what each one means to you.

________	________	________	________	________

________	________	________	________	________

A New Emoji

If you could create a new emoji, what would it be? Decide what feeling you want your emoji to show. Draw your emoji below.

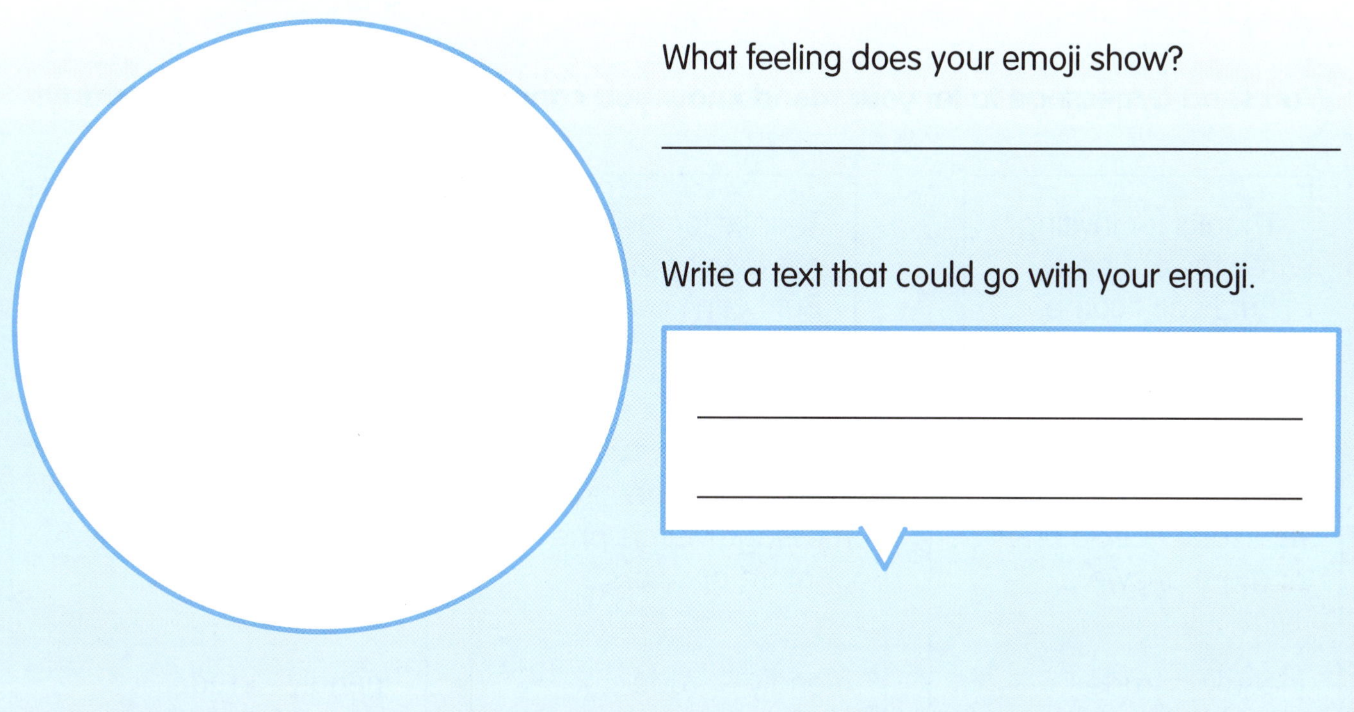

Draw two of your favorite emojis or pictures that you've seen people use.

What's the Tone?

Emojis can sometimes change the tone of a message. Punctuation can also change the tone of a message. Look at the examples below. What's the difference?

You send a message to let your friend know you cannot make it to his birthday party:

Thanks for inviting me to your party. But I can't come.	Thanks for inviting me to your party!!! But I can't come. 😭	Thanks for inviting me to your party! But I can't come. 😡
What's the tone of this message? Circle one or more answers.	What's the tone of this message? Circle one or more answers.	What's the tone of this message? Circle one or more answers.
friendly rude	friendly rude	friendly rude
sarcastic excited	sarcastic excited	sarcastic excited
uncaring disappointed	uncaring disappointed	uncaring disappointed
Write your own tone: ______	Write your own tone: ______	Write your own tone: ______

Tell which message you would send, or write a different message.

____

____

____

You send a message to ask a friend to come over to your house to play:

Hey. Do you want to come over to my house to play?

Hey!!! 😀 Do you want to come over to my house to play??

Hey! Do you want to come over to my house to play? 🤔

What's the tone of this message?

____

____

What's the tone of this message?

____

____

What's the tone of this message?

____

____

Which message would you send? Circle it.

You send a message to let someone know what you thought of his or her joke.

Haha. That is the funniest thing I've ever heard.

Haha! 😂 That is the funniest thing I've ever heard. 😂 😂

Haha. That is the funniest thing I've ever heard. 🙄

What's the tone of this message?

____

____

What's the tone of this message?

____

____

What's the tone of this message?

____

____

Which message would you send? Circle it.

Should I Send It?

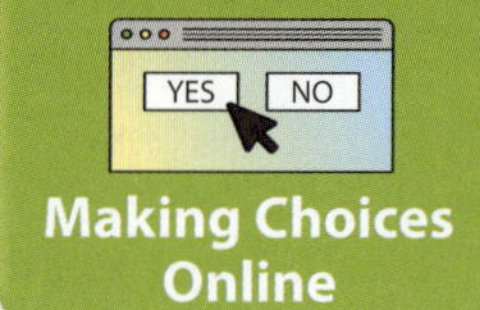

Making Choices Online

Sometimes online, you might get a picture from someone and wonder if it is okay to share with more people. Sometimes it may be okay to share pictures, and sometimes it may not be okay. If you aren't sure, you can ask permission first. You can also ask for help from your family.

Read about each situation. Look at the photo. Decide whether you would share it with others. Color the button to show your answer. Then explain why you chose your answer.

Your friend Germaine e-mails you a photo. It shows him standing by his family's brand-new house. The house number is in the photo.

Would you post this photo on social media?

I would ask Germaine first.

Why did you choose this answer?

____

____

____

____

____

____

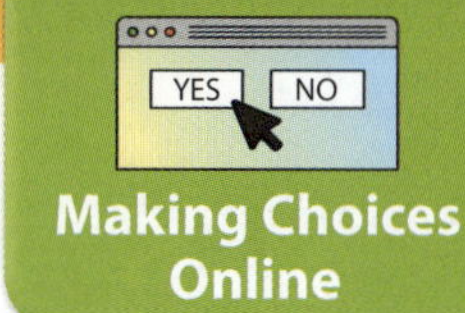

Your friend Nellie texts you a photo. It shows Nellie frowning and looking annoyed. Her little sister is making a silly face.

Would you send this photo to five other friends on a group text?

I would ask Nellie and her sister first.

Why did you choose this answer?

____

____

You are at a slumber party. You take a photo of your friends in their pajamas.

Would you e-mail this photo to friends who weren't at the party?

I would ask the friends who are in the picture first.

Why did you choose this answer?

____

____

Making Choices Online

Talk with Your Family

Is It Okay?

When you are online, you might have to make some hard choices. Your family can help you figure out how to make choices that are respectful of others and that keep you safe.

Read the questions below with your parents. Talk about the answers.

 Is it okay to share pictures of people if I get their permission first?

 Is it okay to e-mail or text my address to others?

 Is it okay to send a picture that shows my address or location?

 What kinds of pictures, e-mails, and texts are okay to send to friends? Are there some types of pictures, e-mails, and texts that I shouldn't send to friends?

 What kinds of pictures, e-mails, and texts are okay to send to family? Are there some types of pictures, e-mails, and texts that I shouldn't send to family?

Cause and Effect

Sometimes sharing a photo can be fun. Other times, sharing might not be the best choice. You can think about possible effects before you share a photo.

Draw lines matching each **cause** to the most likely **effect.**

Cause	Effect
My friend sent me a picture of herself winning first place in a cross-country race. I sent it to another close friend of ours. I copied my friend on the text so she knew I sent it.	My friend got angry and asked why I shared the photo.
I took a picture of my friend when he was in the nurse's office at school. He looked really sweaty and pale in the picture. I thought it was funny so I posted it on social media.	My friend thanked me for sharing the photo.
My friend sent me a photo of his address so I could mail him a package. I asked if I could share the photo with another friend of ours.	My friend said, "Yes, that's fine."

Read the cause below. Then write what you think the effect might be.

My friend sent me a photo of herself with a new haircut. She sent the photo with a text that said, "Don't I look terrible?" She seemed really upset. I shared the photo with four other friends from our class.

____

____

____

The Best Audience

Sometimes people share photos just with friends or with family. Other times, people may share photos more widely, with people they don't know. You can figure out the best audience for your photos. Or you can decide that you don't want to share a photo at all.

Think about what kind of photos you would or wouldn't share with friends, family, or everyone on the Internet. Look at the audience for each photo. Draw an example of a photo you might share with that person or group. If you wouldn't share any photos with that audience, write **NONE** in the box. Then write why you wouldn't share.

Audience: My closest friend

Audience: My family

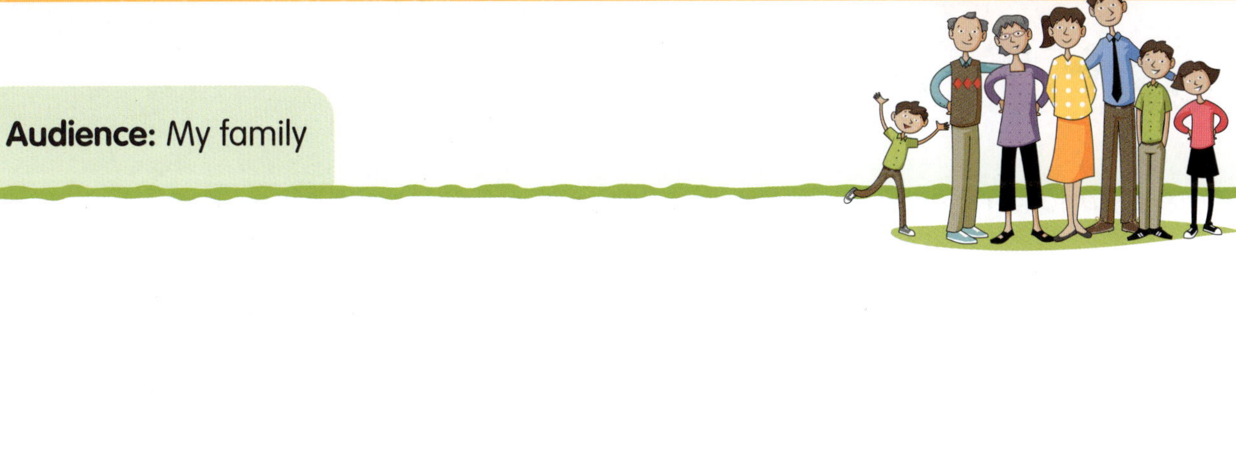

Audience: Everyone on the Internet

Post It?

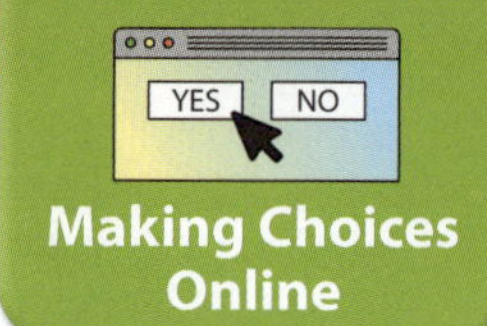

Some information is okay to post online. Some information might be unsafe.

Look at the information in the speech bubbles on the computer screen below. Draw a star in the speech bubbles that tell something you would post online for everyone on the Internet to see, including people you don't know. Draw an **X** through the information you would not post online.

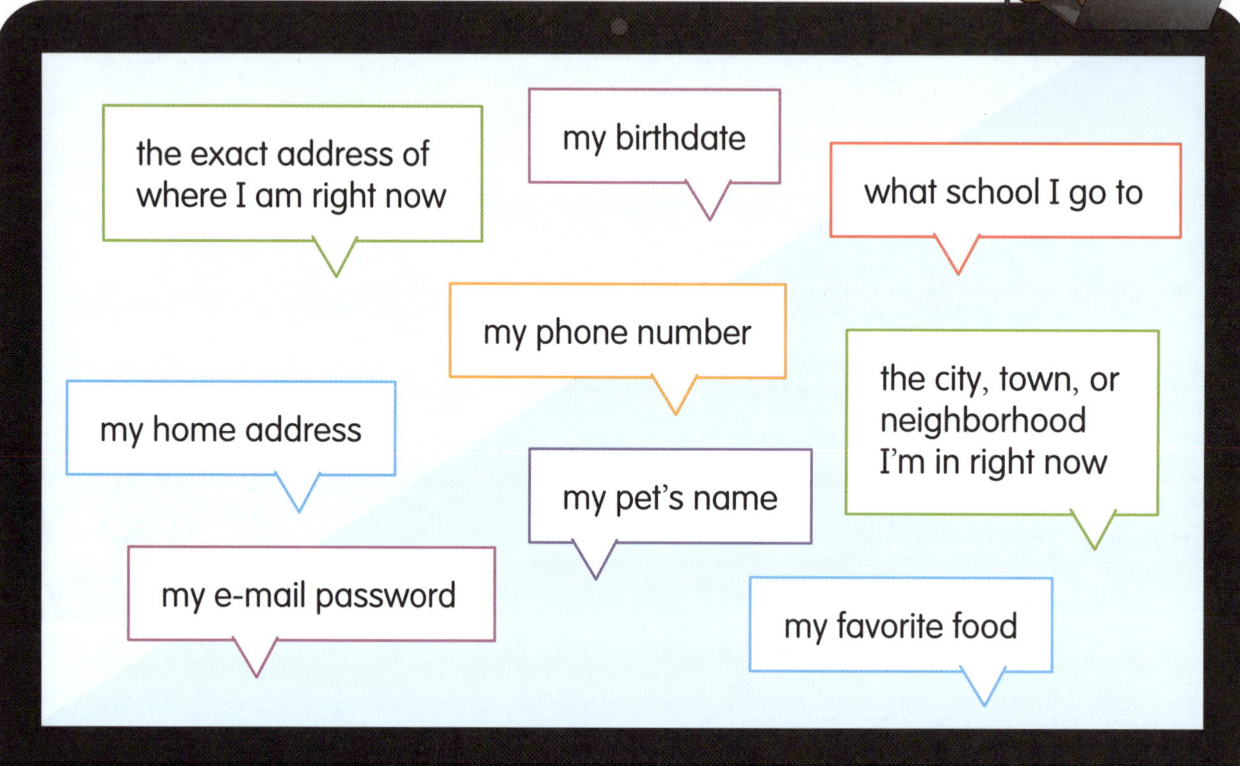

Compare Your Answers

Ask an adult family member to look at your answers. Ask if his or her answers would be different or the same. If the answers are different, ask why.

Your Feelings Online

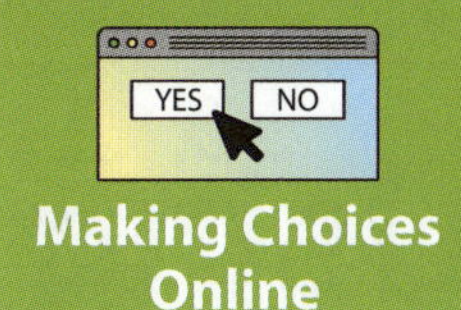

It is important to think about your feelings whenever you are online or on an app. If you notice that any activity on a computer or phone is making you feel unhappy or not okay, then try to stop the activity.

Read about each situation. Then answer the question.

Kyrie read a story online about one of his favorite athletes, and it wasn't very nice. Then Kyrie clicked on **Comments** to read what other people who read the article were saying. Most of the comments were mean, but they made Kyrie laugh. So Kyrie started to type a mean comment, too. Before he hit **Post**, he thought, "Wait, does posting this make me an online troll?" Trolls bully people online and try to make people feel bad about themselves. Kyrie didn't like the idea of being a troll, but he also wanted to join in the conversation online.

What do you think Kyrie should do and why?

Juno was looking at online pictures of people she knew. One girl was on vacation in Hawaii. A boy got new shoes and was showing them off. Her neighbor Irving had a big birthday party. A girl she knew got a puppy. "Wow, everyone else is so lucky," Juno thought. "What's special about me?" Juno felt like crying. Her dad noticed she was upset and asked why. He listened. Then he told her not to compare herself to other people. "I guess you're right," said Juno. "I have a dog, a cat, and a fish. Some people might think that's pretty cool. Maybe I'll post some pics of my pets."

Do you agree with Juno's dad's advice? Why or why not?

Using Social Media to Be Positive

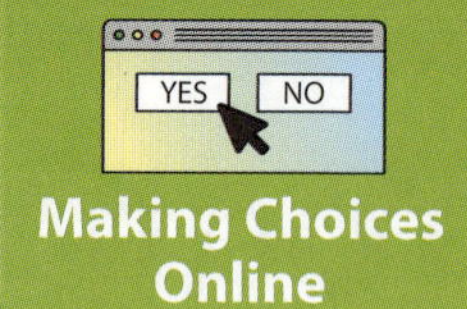

There are a lot of ways to use social media. People can use social media to do things that they think are positive. When something is positive, it is helpful, cheerful, confident, or hopeful.

Read about the things that people can use social media for. In each triangle, draw a 😊 if you think it tells something positive. Draw a 🙁 if you think it tells something that is not positive.

You can use social media to...

- give a friend a compliment
- get information and learn
- stay in touch with friends and family
- show your activity
- make fun of someone
- waste time on stuff you don't think is that important

Note: Cut apart the pages. Put them in order. Staple them together.

staple

staple

My Social Skills

Handbook

CONTENTS

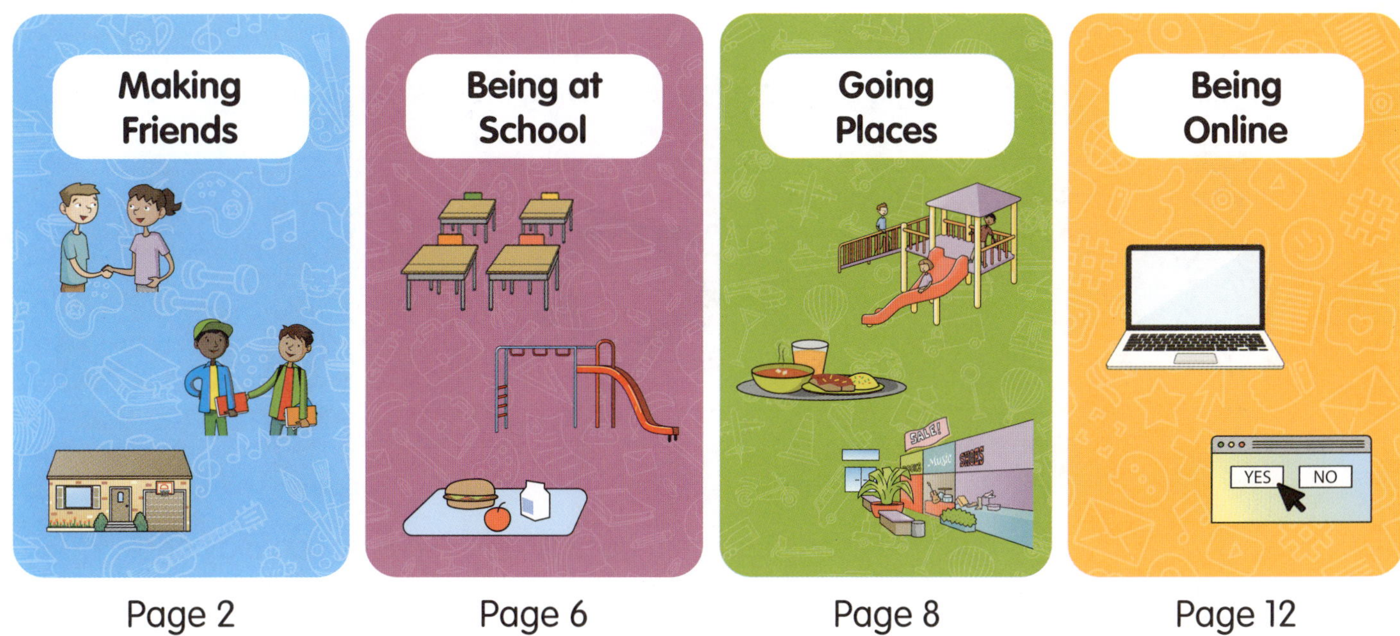

You are learning about social skills. Good for you!

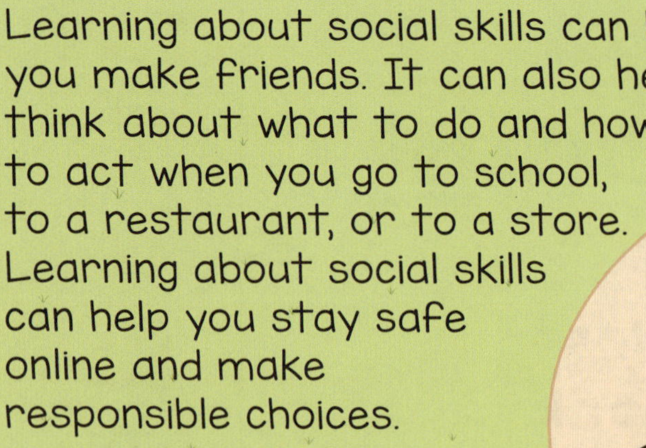

Learning about social skills can help you make friends. It can also help you think about what to do and how to act when you go to school, to a restaurant, or to a store. Learning about social skills can help you stay safe online and make responsible choices.

You can look at this handbook to remind you of what you learned about social skills.

Friendship Is Important

Everyone needs a friend. Anyone can be a friend. Having friends is important.

Friends can talk to each other.

Friends can help each other with problems.

Friends can play and laugh together.

Meeting a New Friend

When you meet someone new, you introduce yourself. Sometimes it is hard to think of what else to say. There are things you can say to make it easier to talk to people.

You can say, "Hi! What's your name?"

You can ask a question.

You can say something nice.

Explaining Rules and Boundaries

Families have different rules and people have different boundaries. You can feel comfortable telling a friend the rules at your house and your boundaries.

We can play at the park. We just need to ask first.

We need to wait until after dinner to have cookies.

I like to share, but please ask before you borrow my things.

Being a Friend

Friends treat each other well and show kindness to each other. But sometimes friends disagree or hurt each other's feelings. Friends talk to each other about their feelings.

I'm sorry I hurt your feelings. I won't do that again.

I feel nervous about the test. Can you help me study?

I like how our fort turned out! We make a good team!

Making Choices at School

You will make many choices when you are at school. Some of the choices will be easy to make. Others may be difficult. It is important to think about your choices.

I feel upset about what happened.

You can choose to respect others whether you are happy or upset.

1...2...3...

You can choose how to react when you are angry.

You can choose to keep yourself and others healthy.

Being a Good Classmate

You spend a lot of time with your classmates. You share the same classroom and the things in the classroom. There are things you can do to be a good classmate.

Respect other people's belongings.

Listen when other people are speaking.

Don't make fun of others or bully them.

Seeing People When You Go Places

You see many different people when you go places. Every person looks different, feels differently, and thinks differently. Remember these things when you see people.

Do not assume a person needs help because he or she has a disability.

Do not make assumptions about people based on how they look.

It is okay to be curious about or interested in how a person looks.

Greeting People When You Go Places

There are many ways to greet people when you go places.

You can look at the person and say "hi."

You can give a fist bump.

You can shake hands.

Going to a Store

When you go to a store, you think about how to act, what to do, and what choices you can make. You might think about these things:

how to ask a person who works at the store a question

how to stand in line and pay for your purchase

how your behavior affects other people in the store

Going to a Restaurant

When you go to a restaurant, you think about how to act, what to do, and what choices you can make. You might think about these things:

how to order food from a server

how to handle things that happen such as getting the wrong order

how your behavior affects other people in the restaurant

Having Digital Respect

It is important to think about your digital-respect list before you send a message or share a photo or video online.

Think about how the person receiving the message will feel.

Make sure you have permission to share photos or videos.

Make sure you are sharing a message only with people you trust.

Being Safe Online

When you share information or pictures online, you think about whether it is safe. Some personal details should be shared only with your family or friends.

I share my full name and birthday only with a friend.

I ask before I share photos that show others.

Talk to your parents about whom you can trust online.